Blended Family *Blueprint*

THE ULTIMATE GUIDE TO OVERCOMING
OBSTACLES AS A BLENDED FAMILY
+ Easy Strategies to Finding Peace and Happiness

By Tyi & Michael Simpson

DISCLAIMER

The advice contained in this material might not be suitable for everyone. The authors designed the information to present their opinion about the subject matter. The reader must carefully investigate all aspects of any family, finance, or business decision before committing to him or herself. The authors obtained the information contained herein from sources they believe to be reliable and from their own personal experience, but they neither imply nor intend any guarantee of accuracy. The authors are not in the business of giving legal, accounting, or any other type of professional advice. Should the reader need such advice, he or she must seek services from a competent professional. The authors particularly disclaim any liability, loss, or risk taken by individuals who directly or indirectly act on the information contained herein. The authors believe the advice presented here is sound, but readers cannot hold them responsible for either the actions they take, or the risk taken by individuals who directly or indirectly act on the information contained herein.

Published by This Thing Publishing
Printed in the United States
Copyright © 2023 by Tyi & Michael Simpson
ISBN 979-8988805304

Dedication

This book is dedicated to the magical power of blending – a force that unites the seemingly incompatible, creating a beautiful mosaic of love and unity from a fascinating array of unique pieces.

This book is more than a guide; it is our hope for all blended families navigating their unique journeys. We dream that our shared experiences and lessons will serve as a beacon of hope, illuminating the path towards unity, understanding, and enduring love in blended families everywhere. This is for all of you.

Acknowledgements

This book, much like the journey it details, would not have been possible without the involvement, love, and support of many remarkable people. To all who have been a part of our story and those who've helped us to tell it, we extend our deepest gratitude.

To each other, for being not just partners in life but also co-authors in this beautiful narrative of our blended family. Our meeting was serendipitous, our love transformative, and our journey together a blueprint for the guidance we now provide to others. Each day, we continue to learn, grow, and cherish the love we share - a love that has healed and fortified us in unimaginable ways.

To our parents, Elfrida Nowell, Fay Simpson, Andre Simpson, and Carnell Joyner, who bestowed upon us valuable wisdom and strength, particularly the distinct resilience borne of a West Indian upbringing. You instilled in us hard lessons and immeasurable skills, which inadvertently guided us towards each other and formed the foundation of our unified family.

To our extraordinary children, who are the essence of our story and the inspiration for this book:

- Imani, with your bold spirit, independent mind, and unwavering courage, you've taught us the power of resilience.

- Jelani, our gentle giant, you embody the essence of an eldest brother and son, demonstrating strength and power in your quiet demeanor.
- Sekai, your infectious smile brightens every room, and your indomitable spirit is a testament to your strength.
- Jayden, the baby boy, your simplicity and purity remind us of the beauty in life's basics.
- Sarae Tahani, our warrior Taurus, your extraordinary heart and sharp mind never cease to amaze us.
- Skylah, the one who completes our circle, your curious mind and miraculous heart are the cherries on top of our blended family.

Our village, the amazing community that has been a part of our lives, deserves special mention. Our friends, who are no less than family, have supported and stood by us through thick and thin. Your presence in our lives is a blessing, and we are eternally grateful for your unwavering support.

Lastly, to Ash Cash Exantus, our mentor, whose invaluable guidance and insights have been instrumental in making this book a reality. You saw our vision and helped bring it to light in a way that surpasses our wildest dreams.

This book is a testament to all of you. It stands as a tribute to the power of love, understanding, resilience, and family. We are grateful to you all, and we share this accomplishment with you. Thank you for being a part of our blissfully blended journey.

Table of Contents

INTRODUCTION

Blended families face an array of challenges as they forge new relationships and unite to form a cohesive family unit. Children may struggle to adapt to their bonus parents or bonus siblings, while parents navigate new roles and boundaries. In this context, using terms like "bonus parents" and "bonus children" instead of "stepparents" and "stepchildren" can foster a more positive and inclusive environment, emphasizing the additional love and support that these new family members bring to the table. Loyalty conflicts can emerge, leading children to feel torn between biological parents and stepparents, and parents striving to balance the needs of their old and new families. Communication breakdowns and misunderstandings may arise from differing styles and expectations. Moreover, blended families may grapple with complex financial arrangements, diverse parenting styles, jealousy and resentment among children, inconsistent discipline, unresolved issues from previous marriages, and intricate relationships with ex-spouses, including co-parenting arrangements and visitation schedules. Cultural and religious differences can also generate tension, necessitating compromise and understanding. Successfully overcoming these challenges requires a strong commitment to open communication, mutual respect, and a shared determination to work together as a family.

We are Michael and Tyi Simpson, experts in blending families, and we're here to help you navigate and overcome the challenges that arise when bringing families together. Drawing from our own experiences in merging a family, we have developed a wealth of solutions that have yielded positive results. Our mission is to debunk common myths surrounding blended families and provide a solution-based framework to help you, step by step, blend your family harmoniously.

By the end of this book, you will be equipped to engage in meaningful dialogue with all the parents and guardians involved, focusing on creating a blissfully blended family that benefits both the adults and children.

Our blended family holds a distinct, intricate charm. Over the years, we've shaped and reshaped our unique family tree, each member playing an integral role in its continual evolution.

Tyi, the matriarch of our clan, embarked on her journey into the world of blended families at the tender age of 20. From her early marriage, she embraced the role of a bonus parent, caring for a one-year-old girl as her own. Now, nearly three decades later, this girl, an essential branch of our family tree, has grown into a woman of 29. She's woven into the very fabric of our family narrative, despite our current estrangement due to a misunderstanding three years ago. She's always considered, always a part of us - a testament to the resilience of love and bonds that transcend bloodlines.

The blend of our family extended when Tyi gave birth to four children during her previous marriage. So, when Michael entered our lives, he willingly accepted not only Tyi but also her rich tapestry of five children - three boys and two girls. The family blend took on a new hue with the arrival of our youngest, Skylah. This spirited five-year-old has a magical ability to bind us all together, further enriching our complex, beautiful family structure.

Tyi's experience of being both the biological parent and a bonus parent brings a nuanced perspective to our family dynamics. She knows what it feels like to love a child that's not her own and to share her biological children's love with a bonus parent. Michael, her present partner & best friend, is a testament to the power of acceptance and love, as he's embraced not only Tyi's four children but also the bonus child from Tyi's first marriage. His ability to navigate the terrain of a blended family with grace is truly admirable.

Our family isn't exempt from the hurdles that come with blending lives, histories, and personalities. Yet, we've learned that love, our greatest asset, has the power to overcome any obstacle. It's the universal language that smooths over our differences and binds us together, creating a unique blend that's our own.

Extended relatives on both sides have graciously erased the lines of separation, adopting each child as their own. Grandparents, godparents, aunts, and uncles - everyone has contributed to weaving the vibrant, colorful tapestry of our family. Michael's parents treat every grandchild as their own, and his siblings dote on the children as their nieces and nephews. There's no "yours" or "mine" in our family - only "ours."

In our family, the children know nothing of separation. They've grown up in an environment where everyone is treated equally, and every relationship is valued. It's this unity, this lack of separation, that makes us cherish our blended family.

Indeed, each blended family is a mosaic of unique pieces, each contributing to a beautiful, shared whole. Ours is a testament to this beautiful reality. As we navigate through our story, we welcome you to explore the delightful complexities and infinite love that defines our blended family.

Our ultimate aim is to facilitate the creation of a cohesive family unit, both within and outside the home, that moves peacefully and cooperatively through life. This blended family blueprint is designed to help all types of families, whether you are a biological parent living with the children or a "bonus" parent looking to build a relationship with them. This honest guide encourages blending different styles and fostering smooth transitions for everyone involved.

We will help you peel back the layers and provide a roadmap for your unique blended family journey. By following our programs and guidance from the Blissful Family Academy, you will focus on relationship building and living in the present. Our approach promotes authenticity in your requests and relationships, encouraging continued work towards the ultimate goal: a blissfully blended family.

Fourteen years ago, we began our blended family journey. Along the way, we faced numerous challenges that we hope to spare you from experiencing. We understand the difficulties in addressing financial contributions, dividing time and responsibilities both inside and outside the home, and determining roles and boundaries for parents. We know the importance of building relationships among all parties involved, and we're here to share our wisdom on overcoming these challenges.

In the past, popular culture often depicted blended families as either harmonious, like the Brady Bunch, or fraught with wicked stepparents and conniving stepchildren. Today's blended families are diverse and multifaceted, reflecting changes in social norms and values. To help you navigate these complexities, we will provide step-by-step guidance on:

- Establishing open lines of communication with all family members.
- Identifying conflicts and areas of common ground.
- Setting realistic family goals.
- Creating a plan to address conflicts and promote cooperation.

- Building respect among family members.
- Accepting and accommodating differences.
- Fostering bonding through shared activities and traditions.
- Seeking professional help when needed.

To ensure success in implementing our solutions, it's crucial to avoid common mistakes that can undermine the harmony and cohesion of a blended family. By being aware of these potential pitfalls, you can proactively address them and create an environment where everyone feels valued and supported.

1. Favoritism: It's natural to have a special bond with your biological children, but showing favoritism can lead to resentment and jealousy among other family members. Treat all children fairly and equitably, offering praise, attention, and discipline consistently to avoid creating rifts within the family.
2. Rushing the blending process: Integrating two families takes time, and it's essential to be patient with the process. Allowing everyone the space to adjust at their own pace will foster a more harmonious environment and encourage healthy relationships to develop.
3. Ignoring individual needs: Each family member will have unique needs, feelings, and experiences that must be acknowledged and addressed. Be empathetic and compassionate, making an effort to understand each person's perspective and offer support when needed.
4. Neglecting the couple relationship: In a blended family, it's essential to prioritize the relationship between the two partners. Spending quality time together, maintaining open communication, and working together as a team will help create a strong foundation for the family.

5. Disregarding the role of the ex-partner: It's important to acknowledge and respect the relationship between your partner's children and their other parent. Encourage open communication and maintain a civil relationship with the ex-partner for the sake of the children.

6. Inconsistent rules and expectations: Establishing clear and consistent rules and expectations for all family members helps create a sense of stability and predictability. Ensure that all adults are on the same page and work together to enforce these expectations.

7. Overlooking the importance of self-care: Blending families can be emotionally and physically demanding. Prioritizing self-care for each family member, including the adults, will help maintain mental and emotional wellbeing, which ultimately benefits the entire family.

Blended families, often called bonus families, are increasingly becoming a common family structure in our society. This term is a broad, encompassing phrase to describe families that are born out of two or more separate family units coming together. This could be a result of remarriage, cohabitation or other circumstances where children from previous relationships are introduced to new parental figures and potential siblings. The concept of a blended family is not new, yet it's more relevant than ever as our societal norms evolve and the traditional nuclear family structure diversifies. This chapter aims to explore the definition of blended families, their prevalence and statistics, and the importance of addressing the unique challenges they face.

The composition of families has significantly shifted over the past few decades, with blended families becoming more common. According to data from the U.S. Census Bureau, over 16% of children live in what would be classified as blended families. This shows the growing prevalence of such family structures, reflecting societal changes and evolving attitudes towards marriage, divorce, and cohabitation.

These families can be formed in several ways. For instance, they can arise when single parents from previous relationships marry, bringing their children into a new, combined household. They can also form when a person with children marries someone without children, introducing a new parent into the mix. In some cases, both parents might bring children from previous relationships into their new family unit.

The prevalence of blended families varies across different demographics and geographical areas. Factors such as socioeconomic status, cultural norms, and regional attitudes towards divorce and remarriage can influence the frequency of blended families. For instance, blended families are more prevalent in urban areas compared to rural areas, likely due to more progressive attitudes towards family structures.

However, these statistics only provide a snapshot of the current situation. As societal attitudes continue to evolve, the prevalence of blended families is likely to increase in the future. This changing family dynamic underlines the importance of understanding and addressing the unique challenges faced by blended families.

Blended families, while offering many benefits, also face unique challenges. These range from interpersonal conflicts and boundary issues to logistical complications and legal concerns. Addressing these challenges is crucial not only for the wellbeing of the individual family members but also for the stability of our wider society.

Children in blended families might struggle to adjust to new parental figures or siblings. They may experience feelings of confusion, jealousy, or resentment, which can lead to behavioral issues if not addressed properly. Parents, on the other hand, might face difficulties in defining their roles and responsibilities, managing relationships with former partners, and creating a harmonious home environment.

Beyond the personal sphere, these challenges can also have wider societal implications. For example, children from blended families who struggle with academic performance due to family-related stress could contribute to lower overall educational outcomes. Similarly, legal disputes related to blended families can put a strain on the judicial system.

Therefore, it's critical to address these challenges through various means. This could involve providing psychological support for children, offering parenting guidance for adults, and implementing policy changes to better accommodate the needs of blended families. By addressing these challenges, we can help ensure that every family, regardless of its structure, has the opportunity to thrive.

By being mindful of these common mistakes and working together to create a supportive and nurturing environment, blended families can overcome the unique challenges they face and build strong, lasting relationships with one another.

Blended families, often called bonus families, are increasingly becoming a common family structure in our society. This term is a broad, encompassing phrase that describes families born out of two or more separate family units coming together. This could be a result of remarriage, cohabitation, or other circumstances where children from previous relationships are introduced to new parental figures and potential siblings. The concept of a blended family is not new, yet it is more relevant than ever as our societal norms evolve and the traditional nuclear family structure diversifies. This chapter aims to explore the definition of blended families, their prevalence and statistics, and the importance of addressing the unique challenges they face.

The composition of families has significantly shifted over the past few decades, with blended families becoming more common. According to data from the U.S. Census Bureau, over 16% of children live in what would be classified as blended families. This shows the growing prevalence of such family structures, reflecting societal changes and evolving attitudes towards marriage, divorce, and cohabitation.

These families can be formed in several ways. For instance, they can arise when single parents from previous relationships marry, bringing their children into a new, combined household. They can also form when a person with children marries someone without children, introducing a new parent into the mix. In some cases, both parents might bring children from previous relationships into their new family unit.

The prevalence of blended families varies across different demographics and geographical areas. Factors such as socioeconomic status, cultural norms, and regional attitudes towards divorce and remarriage can influence the frequency of blended families. For instance, blended families are more prevalent in urban areas compared to rural areas, likely due to more progressive attitudes towards family structures.

However, these statistics only provide a snapshot of the current situation. As societal attitudes continue to evolve, the prevalence of blended families is likely to increase in the future. This changing family dynamic underlines the importance of understanding and addressing the unique challenges faced by blended families.

Blended families, while offering many benefits, also face unique challenges. These range from interpersonal conflicts and boundary issues to logistical complications and legal concerns. Addressing these challenges is crucial not only for the wellbeing of the individual family members but also for the stability of our wider society.

Children in blended families might struggle to adjust to new parental figures or siblings. They may experience feelings of confusion, jealousy, or resentment, which can lead to behavioral issues if not addressed properly. Parents, on the other hand, might face difficulties in defining their roles and responsibilities, managing relationships with former partners, and creating a harmonious home environment.

Beyond the personal sphere, these challenges can also have wider societal implications. For example, children from blended families who struggle with academic performance due to family-related stress could contribute to lower overall educational outcomes. Similarly, legal disputes related to blended families can put a strain on the judicial system.

Therefore, it is critical to address these challenges through various means. This could involve providing psychological support for children, offering parenting guidance for adults, and implementing policy changes to better accommodate the needs of blended families. By addressing these challenges, we can help ensure that every family, regardless of its structure, has the opportunity to thrive.

CHAPTER I

UNDERSTANDING THE CHALLENGES OF BLENDED FAMILIES

Blended families, while becoming more common and widely accepted, often face a unique set of challenges. These families, composed of bonus parents and bonus children, must navigate a complex landscape of emotions, relationships, and societal norms. By understanding the difficulties that may arise, blended families can better equip themselves with strategies and tools to manage these issues and thrive together.

The very inception of our blended family was a challenge in itself. Tyi and I managed to date for three whole years before her children were introduced to our relationship. We shared a workplace, so her children knew me, but they didn't connect the dots that Tyi and I were dating. They viewed me as "Mr. Whatever," a friendly face at their mom's job, while remaining blissfully unaware of the burgeoning romance.

Dating in discretion was our initial choice; we wanted to ensure the bond we were nurturing was real, with the potential for a shared future. However, blending our family was not as smooth as we had anticipated. Our first attempt was a bowling trip - an opportunity for the kids to interact with me outside of the workspace. But as the day approached, I got cold feet, pulling out from the trip at the last moment. The fear of stepping into the bonus parent role was overwhelming.

Following this, we planned a dinner outing, and yet again, I bailed, unable to embrace the change. My hesitations were authentic, but they also caused hurt. Clear about our feelings but stuck at a crossroads, we took a break from each other for three months.

It was a difficult period of introspection and decision-making, which culminated in a 'come to Jesus' moment—a seven-hour long conversation dissecting our fears, aspirations, and expectations from the future. During this discussion, I conveyed my concerns about becoming a bonus parent. I was apprehensive about forming relationships with Tyi's children, only to potentially cause pain if our relationship didn't work out. I admired her children already but didn't want to risk causing any distress to them or myself.

This instance emphasized the importance of open communication in overcoming the challenges we faced. Tyi's determination and confidence in our relationship eventually assured me to take a leap of faith into this new chapter of our lives. She was resolute about moving forward, and I learned to trust her instincts.

The early stages of blending our family were punctuated by these moments of doubt and uncertainty. External reassurance from a friend finally nudged us past our inhibitions. Their perspective highlighted the special bond Tyi and I shared, pushing us to overcome the hurdles that stood in our way.

Finally, three years into our relationship, I met Tyi's children officially as their mom's boyfriend, marking a significant milestone in our journey.

Keeping our relationship under wraps at work and maintaining distance from Tyi's kids had indeed been challenging, but our open communication ultimately saw us through. Our first bowling trip was eventually rescheduled and turned out to be a wonderful day, solidifying the bonds that were just beginning to form.

Our journey into becoming a blended family was marked by trials and challenges, but it was our communication and love for each other that navigated us through the storm. And here we are today, a testament to our determination and unwavering love for each other and our blended family.....

The caveat to blending this family was that Michael was willing. He was willing to listen, he was willing to understand, willing to take advise on each kid and he was willing to take action - slower than I had liked sometimes but willing. He heard when I said, Imani will love you if you treat me right, the way to Jelani's heart is through jokes, Sekai is a hard nut to crack, Jayden just needs hugs & Sarae, well I didn't have to give much instruction - she charmed him at every turn. I had watched Michael with his nieces and knew he was a girl dad. I knew he would build with them easier than the boys. Respecting the children as humans was always a high priority for me and we talked about it before he met them. My famous line is "they came through me but they do not belong to me". For Michael this was a hard one, not that he couldn't respect them but growing up West Indian- as we both did- children are not seen or heard, so navigating a household where the kid's feelings are considered but with it some hearty communication, we were able to toe the line. Once again though, love and understanding prevailed. He would always say, these kids are amazing so why would I change what you've been doing, clearly, it's been working!

Navigating the journey of a blended family, however, brings us to a broader perspective. Across the spectrum, blended families often encounter shared challenges. These difficulties emerge from various facets, including defining new family roles, reconciling different parenting styles, managing shared living spaces, and processing a gamut of emotions.

Bonus parents may find it difficult to strike a balance between being an authority figure and a friend, while bonus children may struggle with divided loyalties or feelings of being an outsider in their own home. The establishment of new relationships, coupled with the dissolution of previous ones, can also create friction within the family.

Moreover, the merging of different parenting styles can pose a challenge. Discrepancies in disciplinary tactics, household rules, and expectations can lead to confusion and conflict. Similarly, the sharing of physical spaces like bedrooms, bathrooms, and common areas can cause tension, especially when privacy issues arise.

Blended families face unique challenges mainly because they are formed under circumstances that involve significant changes to the original family structures. The process of blending two separate families involves integrating different histories, traditions, parenting styles, and sometimes, cultural or socioeconomic backgrounds.

Additionally, blended families often have to deal with external factors such as societal expectations and legal issues. For example, the societal portrayal of a 'typical' family can lead to feelings of isolation or 'otherness'. Legal matters related to custody, visitation rights, or financial responsibilities can further complicate the family dynamics.

The challenges encountered by blended families can have a profound impact on the family as a whole, as well as on individual family members. It can affect the mental and emotional well-being of the family members, strain relationships, and create a tense home environment.

Children, especially, can feel the effects deeply. They might exhibit behavioral issues, academic problems, or signs of depression or anxiety. Parents, on the other hand, may experience feelings of guilt, frustration, or helplessness if they're unable to successfully integrate the family.

However, it is important to remember that these challenges also have the potential to strengthen the family unit. Overcoming adversity can foster resilience, teach important life skills, and deepen family bonds. The key lies in understanding these challenges, openly addressing them, and seeking help when necessary.

In conclusion, acknowledging and understanding these challenges is the first step towards addressing them. By doing so, blended families can pave the way for stronger relationships, improved communication, and a more harmonious home environment. The journey may be difficult at times, but the formation of a loving, supportive blended family is a reward that far outweighs the trials faced along the way.

Action Steps for Chapter I

1.1 Understanding the Blended Family Structure

Activity: Draw a family tree including all members of the blended family. Make sure to include bonus parents and bonus children, reflecting the inclusive language of the family.

Reflection: Write a paragraph on how this blended family structure makes you feel. Are there challenges you foresee? What are the positive aspects?

_____

_____

_____

_____

_____

_____

_____

_____

_____

_____

_____

_____

_____

_____

_____

_____

_____

_____

_____

_____

_____

_____

_____

1.2 Understanding Prevalence and Normalization

Research: Look up and jot down statistics about blended families. How common is your situation?

_____

_____

_____

_____

_____

_____

_____

_____

_____

_____

_____

_____

_____

_____

_____

_____

_____

_____

_____

_____

_____

_____

_____

Reflection: How do these statistics make you feel? Do they provide a sense of normality? Discuss this in your family group.

_____

_____

_____

_____

_____

_____

_____

_____

_____

_____

_____

_____

_____

_____

_____

_____

_____

_____

_____

_____

_____

_____

_____

1.3 Identifying Potential Challenges

Brainstorm: Make a list of potential challenges your blended family might face. They could be issues like sharing space, adjusting to new roles, or dealing with emotions.

Action Plan: Next to each challenge, write down one way you could potentially address it.

_____

_____

_____

_____

_____

_____

_____

_____

_____

_____

_____

_____

_____

_____

_____

_____

_____

_____

_____

1.4 Open Communication

Activity: Hold a family meeting where each member can express their feelings or concerns about the new family structure. Use space below for any notes from your meeting.

_____

_____

_____

_____

_____

_____

_____

_____

_____

_____

_____

_____

_____

_____

_____

_____

_____

_____

_____

_____

Reflection: Write down your thoughts on this meeting. Did any concerns surprise you? What did you learn about your family members?

_____

_____

_____

_____

_____

_____

_____

_____

_____

_____

_____

_____

_____

_____

_____

_____

_____

_____

_____

_____

_____

_____

_____

_____

_____

1.5 Establishing New Roles and Boundaries

Discussion: As a family, talk about roles and responsibilities. Who will take care of chores, help with homework, or organize family activities?

Action Plan: Write down these roles and responsibilities and put them in a place where everyone can see.

_____

_____

_____

_____

_____

_____

_____

_____

_____

_____

_____

_____

_____

_____

_____

_____

_____

_____

_____

_____

1.6 Building Relationships

Activity: Plan a family day where everyone can spend time together and bond. It could be a picnic, movie night, or a day trip.

Reflection: Write about this experience. Did you learn anything new about your family members? How did this activity impact your relationship with them?

_____

_____

_____

_____

_____

_____

_____

_____

_____

_____

_____

_____

_____

_____

_____

_____

_____

_____

_____

1.7 Celebrating Differences

Activity: Each family member should present something that represents their individuality, it could be a favorite book, a hobby, or a personal story.

Reflection: Write down your thoughts on these presentations. Did they help you understand your family members better?

_____

_____

_____

_____

_____

_____

_____

_____

_____

_____

_____

_____

_____

_____

_____

_____

_____

_____

_____

_____

1.8 Seeking Support

Research: Join our Online and Offline Community; Blissful Blended Academy for resources for blended families.

Reflection: Write about any additional resources you found particularly helpful. Share these resources with your family.

_____

_____

_____

_____

_____

_____

_____

_____

_____

_____

_____

_____

_____

_____

_____

_____

_____

Remember, these steps are not a one-time activity but an ongoing process. Repeat and revisit these steps as needed, adjusting them to the specific needs of your blended family. Patience, empathy, and open communication are key in successfully blending a family.

CHAPTER II

ESTABLISHING A FOUNDATION FOR A SUCCESSFUL BLENDED FAMILY

The formation of a blended family represents a fresh start and a new chapter in the lives of everyone involved. This transition, though full of potential, can be fraught with complexities. By establishing a solid foundation, blended families can navigate these complexities and create a harmonious and loving environment. This chapter delves into crucial steps to laying this groundwork, including creating a family vision and mission statement, establishing clear communication channels, and setting realistic expectations.

A vibrant memory from our blended family journey is that of celebrating birthdays. When Tyi and I first started dating, I was unacquainted with the practice of celebrating my birthday with her children. Being childless at the time, I was accustomed to spending my birthdays with friends or partaking in activities I enjoyed. However, Tyi and the kids had other plans.

They put up decorations and got a cake, immersing me into their family traditions. It wasn't exactly a moment of revelation but rather a milestone in mutual understanding and communication. It led to a conversation about the importance of the children celebrating their bonus father. After all, I had always been there for their birthdays, showering them with gifts and love. It was a poignant moment when I realized the significance of the kids' participation in my birthday celebration. Their joy in singing the birthday song for me was infectious, and by the end of the day, everything felt just right.

This episode marked a crucial turning point in establishing our family traditions. We forged a ritual to honor birthdays with a cake and takeout meal, an arrangement that now forms the core of our celebrations. Everyone's birthday is commemorated in this manner, with either the birthday person picking the takeout or the rest of the family surprising them.

The part that Michael forgot to mention was the first time he didn't show up for his birthday "party" and the kids and I went to bed disappointed. Trying to navigate my feeling of disappointment my attempting to maneuver each one of their questions about where he was and why he didn't show took creativity on my part. Some was lying by omission but also the big picture of knowing that I had the power to tarnish his bond with the children by anything I said or did and that wasn't an option. I had to put the whole picture in front of this small moment in time. If this was going to be the last time they ever saw him then by all means I could have gone all in. But it wasn't, so I couldn't. I was clear that he didn't know or understand and that this time he didn't hear me. Although I was hurt, I was also clear that he had listened to me so many times before about matters of children, that eventually this would be no different. Part of blending is building a relationship and communication style with your partner first. It comes in handy later.

Another significant element in solidifying our family foundation was the introduction of vision boards, a practice Tyi had engaged in with the kids before I came into the picture. Although I was unfamiliar with this concept, my eagerness to partake in their activities led to me embracing it wholeheartedly. Over time, this annual activity morphed into a biennial or triennial one, allowing us to reflect on our dreams and aspirations while reevaluating past goals.

Vision boards provided a window into the minds of our children, enabling us to learn about their interests, aspirations, and hobbies. We were often surprised by the revelations these boards brought to light. Our son's adventurous spirit shone through his desire to partake in extreme sports, while our daughter surprised us with her in-depth knowledge about cars. These vision boards served as a conduit for deeper understanding and connection within our blended family.

Our family's engagement with vision boards has grown from a single parent activity to a collective family tradition, cherished by all of us. Witnessing some of our visions come to life has been a rewarding experience. This activity is not only a chance for family bonding, but it also offers insight into each other's lives. We typically accompany these sessions with an ice cream sundae party, rounding off the day with presentations of each person's vision board.

Collecting magazines for the vision boards became a fun scavenger hunt, an additional bonding experience that added to our family lore. It's heartening to think that these traditions, established in our blended family, may carry forward as our children build their own homes. Through open communication, understanding, and love, we have set a solid foundation for our blended family that continues to thrive.

Wow... vision board! So, this was not a hard activity to get my then boyfriend to participate in, but the children actually had to help him along quite a bit.

This was one of the first times I saw Michael vulnerable with the children. They honestly did not leave him much choice. He sat and watched them navigate their vision boards and he was the newbie. He was really stuck about what and how to do the thing. I don't know if he even remembers but each child helped him with something different on his very first board. We talked, laughed and snacked. When they saw that he was stuck they gently cut out phrases or pictures and handed them to him. They started asking him what he liked and encouraged him to "add more". This activity was pivotal in the business of blending. For me it was what we had always done but thinking back, they got to know Michael in a very different way that day. Later that night, he thanked me for the experience and for always including him. Writing about this now brings back a flood of memories and a reminder that life has happened, and we are way past time to work on new vision boards!

Developing a family vision and mission statement can be a powerful tool in guiding the direction of your blended family. This exercise not only sets a clear path forward, but it also fosters unity and shared values.

In crafting your family vision, think about the kind of environment and values you want to foster. What kind of relationships do you wish to build? What kind of memories do you want to create? Your vision should be inspirational and forward-looking.

The mission statement, on the other hand, is about the present. It's a declaration of the core principles that will guide your family's actions and decisions. It should reflect your family's values and serve as a reminder of what is truly important to your family.

Involve all members of the family in this process. This encourages a sense of ownership and commitment to the family's shared goals and values.

Effective and open communication is a cornerstone of any successful family, and it is particularly crucial for blended families. Open lines of communication ensure that everyone feels heard, understood, and valued.

Establish regular family meetings to discuss issues, plans, and feelings. This can be a space where everyone can speak openly and honestly about their experiences, concerns, and suggestions. It's essential that these meetings are conducted in a respectful and supportive manner.

Encourage one-on-one conversations as well. This allows for more intimate and personal discussions and can help to foster individual relationships within the family.

Remember, communication is not just about speaking, it's also about listening. Active listening demonstrates respect and understanding, and can go a long way in building strong, positive relationships.

Coming into a blended family situation with unrealistic expectations can lead to disappointment and frustration. It's essential to understand that forming a cohesive blended family takes time, patience, and effort from all parties involved.

Acknowledge that the journey towards becoming a unified family won't always be smooth. There will be challenges and setbacks along the way, and that's okay. It's all part of the process.

Moreover, understand that relationships and bonds cannot be forced. Allow them to develop naturally over time. This might take longer for some family members than for others, and that's perfectly normal.

Also, remember that it's okay to ask for help. Whether it's from a counselor, therapist, support group, or trusted friends and family, seeking support is a sign of strength and commitment to creating a successful blended family.

In conclusion, by creating a family vision and mission statement, establishing clear communication channels, and setting realistic expectations, you can lay a solid foundation for a successful blended family. It's a journey that requires effort, patience, and plenty of love, but the reward – a harmonious, supportive, and loving family – is worth every step.

Action Steps for Chapter II

2.1 Reflecting on Family Traditions

1. Take some time to write down your current family traditions. What activities, celebrations, or rituals do you share as a family?

_____

_____

_____

_____

_____

_____

_____

_____

_____

_____

_____

_____

_____

_____

_____

_____

_____

_____

_____

_____

2. Reflect on how these traditions contribute to your family dynamics.

_____

_____

_____

_____

_____

_____

_____

_____

_____

_____

_____

_____

3. Are there any new traditions you'd like to establish as a blended family? Write down your ideas and discuss them with your family.

_____

_____

_____

_____

_____

_____

_____

_____

_____

_____

_____

2.2 Creating a Family Vision Board

1. Plan a day where your family can come together to create a family vision board. This should include everyone's hopes, dreams, and aspirations.
2. Collect magazines, photos, and other materials for your board. You can turn the collection process into a fun family scavenger hunt.
3. After creating your vision boards, present them to each other. Discuss what you've each included and why.

Research Activity: Understanding Vision Boards

1. Conduct some research about the purpose and benefits of creating vision boards.
2. Find examples of vision boards online to inspire your family's creation.
3. Research different methods and materials you could use to create your vision boards.

Use space below to take notes:

_____

_____

_____

_____

_____

2.3 Crafting a Family Vision and Mission Statement

1. As a family, discuss what values and environment you'd like to foster in your home.
2. Write down your shared goals and aspirations - this will form your family vision.
3. Then, draft a mission statement reflecting the core principles that will guide your family's actions and decisions.
4. Review these statements together, make any necessary changes, and ensure everyone feels included and heard.

As an example, our family mission statement goes: United in love and respect, our family mission is to cultivate a nurturing and inclusive home where every member feels valued, heard, and loved. Guided by open communication, shared experiences, and mutual understanding, we strive to honor each individual's unique journey and identity, while nurturing strong, unified family bonds. As a blended family, we embrace our diverse backgrounds and experiences as our greatest strength, continually learning and growing from each other. Our mission is to celebrate our journey as a blended family, fostering a sense of belonging and unity amidst our beautiful diversity. Above all, our family is a haven of acceptance, respect, and love, where we honor our shared and individual journeys and build a legacy of unity and harmony for future generations.

_____

_____

_____

_____

_____

2.4 Establishing Communication Channels

1. Discuss as a family when and how you will have regular family meetings. Decide on the structure these meetings will follow.

_____

_____

_____

_____

_____

_____

_____

_____

2. Create a 'family meeting' agreement. This should set out guidelines to ensure that everyone feels safe, heard, and respected during these meetings. See example below:

Family Meeting Agreement

1. **Purpose of the Meetings:** Our family meetings are designed to foster open communication, resolve conflicts, and strengthen our family bonds. They are a space for us to share our thoughts, feelings, and concerns in a respectful and supportive environment.
2. **Respect:** We agree to treat each other with respect at all times. This means listening to each other without interrupting, refraining from making derogatory comments, and using polite language.
3. **Honesty:** We agree to be honest yet thoughtful in our communication. We understand that the truth can sometimes be hard to hear,

but we believe in the value of authenticity. We will strive to be sensitive to others' feelings when expressing our truth.

4. **Confidentiality:** What's discussed in the family meeting stays within the family. We respect each other's privacy and do not share personal matters outside the meeting.

5. **Listening:** We will practice active listening, which means giving our full attention to the person speaking and refraining from formulating responses while they are talking. We recognize that everyone's input is valuable.

6. **Speaking Turns:** Everyone will have an equal opportunity to speak. We agree to avoid interrupting and will provide each family member their turn to express their thoughts.

7. **Handling Disagreements:** We understand that disagreements may occur. When they do, we will handle them respectfully, without resorting to personal attacks or raised voices. We agree to seek compromise and, when necessary, agree to disagree.

8. **Positivity:** We will start each meeting with something positive, such as sharing one good thing that happened to us that week. We believe in the power of positivity and its ability to set a constructive tone for our meetings.

9. **Actionable Items:** If a problem is presented during the meeting, we will work together to come up with potential solutions. We believe in the power of collective problem-solving and the creativity of our family.

10. **Meeting Duration:** We agree to keep our meetings within a set timeframe (for example, no longer than an hour) to ensure everyone remains engaged and focused.

By agreeing to these guidelines, we commit to fostering a family environment that is nurturing, respectful, and inclusive, enhancing our bond as a blended family.

3. Encourage one-on-one conversations between different family members. This can help build individual relationships within the family.

Reflection Activity: Setting Realistic Expectations

1. Reflect individually on what expectations you have for your blended family. Be as honest as possible.
2. As a family, discuss these expectations. Are they realistic? What steps can be taken to meet them?
3. Acknowledge that there may be challenges and setbacks, but these are part of the blending process. How can you support each other when these occur?
4. Identify sources of support outside the family, like counselors, therapists, support groups, or trusted friends. Research options in your local area.

Remember, creating a successful blended family is a journey, not a destination. Patience, understanding, and open communication will be your best tools along the way.

_____

_____

_____

_____

_____

CHAPTER III

BUILDING RELATIONSHIPS IN A BLENDED FAMILY

Building relationships within a bonus family, which is often referred to as a blended family, is much like embarking on a journey that calls for ample time, patience, and understanding. This journey is multi-faceted, encompassing the fostering of bonds between bonus parents and bonus children, strengthening sibling relationships, navigating loyalty conflicts, and creating unity amongst all parents and guardians. The keys to success on this journey are open communication, empathy, and mutual respect. Each step of the way, these are the core values that guide and foster the growth of strong, meaningful relationships within a bonus family.

As I embarked on the journey of becoming part of a blended family, my wife provided me with insights into the personalities of her children. She offered me a heads-up about who might embrace me easily and who could potentially resist my presence, given their loyalty to their biological father. True to her words, the children gravitated towards me as she predicted, with the exception of our second-to-third oldest son.

Our son wasn't outwardly disrespectful; rather, he was a bit more challenging to reach. He harbored some resistance, which made it a bit harder to connect with him. However, with the passage of time, his defenses started to melt away. He became more open and communicative. Today, at the age of 21, our relationship is a testament to patience and resilience. We never end a phone call without expressing our love for each other. He even surprises me with random video calls - quite an adjustment for someone who isn't particularly fond of phone conversations. It's a powerful illustration of how relationships can evolve and deepen over time, provided we give them the space to do so. It is essential not to pressure children to accept a new parent; they need the freedom to navigate this path at their own pace.

A story comes to mind of the two oldest boys being at sleep away camp, when asked who was coming to pick them up. The oldest son responded, "Our Dad" and was corrected by the middle brother," he's not Our dad, he's mom's boyfriend". The oldest grabbed his brother up & quickly reminded him that "our father didn't want to drive however many hours it was to come get us and our bonus dad is, so you better not let me hear you disrespecting him ever again" A mixture of "yeah boyeee" & "thank you for seeing me" are the feelings that I remember.

Initially, there was tension between this son and me. Our interactions were often awkward, filled with silence and brief exchanges, especially during one-on-one times like car rides to football games. Today, while we may not qualify as best friends, we share a bond that's undoubtedly father-son.

Another poignant experience involves my daughter. She started calling me "Dad" early on in our relationship. As a man without biological children, hearing her call me Dad was heartwarming and would brighten my day. However, we noticed a change when she started referring to me as "Papi". As it turned out, her brother, the one I had initial difficulties connecting with, reported to their biological father that she was calling me "Dad". The biological father corrected her, stating that she had only one father. Hence, the switch to "Papi". We remained unaware of these dynamics until much later in our relationship.

When we found out, we had multiple discussions about the situation. It was essential not to make my daughter uncomfortable or force her to do something she wasn't at ease with. If calling me "Papi" made her comfortable, then that was what mattered most. I cherished being called "Papi" as much as "Dad".

A few years later, her brother, now more mature at 18 or 19, came forward with an apology. He confessed to having been wrong in relaying household details to his biological father. He also admitted to having influenced his younger sister's choice of addressing me. He said he had been led to believe that his mother was trying to replace their biological father. As he grew older, he realized this wasn't true, and he apologized to all of us for his actions. It was a touching family moment that allowed us to discuss and address past misunderstandings, ultimately bringing us closer as a blended family. Now that we have Skylah, my middle daughter naturally dips in and out of calling me Dad, although it's not permanent, I hold on to each time she says it.

Dad. The first time Sarae called him dad we both almost pasted out. It came out of nowhere. I remember calling my mom and my best friend to discuss. I was frantic because I did not know how she arrived there. Yes, we had been doing the work, spending the time but we weren't even living together at the time. My brain flooded with the implications. Did I say or do something to coerce her to saying this? Why was she this comfortable? Was it right or wrong? How would everyone react? Both my mom and my best friend reminded me that we had been doing the work and not to question it. I didn't start it so I shouldn't stop it. It was yet another proof that

Michael had made an impact on the lives of the kids. My heart was full and probably skipped a few beats every time she said it. It was so innocent for her, but she doesn't know, she kind of sealed the deal for us. As a biological single mom thinking about a next relationship is hard, emotional, cautious, exasperating but as a mom of five these feelings are literally multiplied. I have friends who didn't get their new guy to blended with their one or two children and relationships diminished. So, the idea that there was a natural meshed, let us know that this thing we were doing was the right thing.

The relationship between a bonus parent and a bonus child is a delicate one that requires careful nurturing. It's an intricate dance of getting to know one another, building trust, and understanding the unique dynamics of the bonus parent-bonus child relationship.

To start with, it's important to remember that building a relationship with a bonus child is not an overnight process. It takes time and should be approached with patience and respect for the child's feelings and pace. One effective strategy is to start slow, beginning with small steps like spending time together doing activities the child enjoys. This shared experience can serve as a bonding opportunity, providing a platform for the bonus parent to show genuine interest in the child's world.

This interest can extend to engaging in conversations about the child's interests, dreams, and concerns. Taking the time to listen to the child and genuinely engage in these discussions can convey a strong message to the child that the bonus parent truly cares about them, which can strengthen the bond between them.

However, it's also crucial to respect the child's feelings. It's perfectly normal for a child to have mixed emotions about the new family arrangement. As a bonus parent, it's important to validate these feelings and provide the child with the space they need to process their emotions. This respect for their feelings can go a long way in building trust and understanding.

Finally, consistency is key in any relationship, and it's no different in the bonus parent-bonus child relationship. Consistency in behavior, rules, and responses helps to build trust and respect, which are critical foundations for a strong relationship.

Sibling relationships within a bonus family can be complicated, but they are a crucial part of the family dynamics. Fostering strong bonds between siblings can help to strengthen the family as a whole and create a more harmonious family environment.

One strategy for building strong sibling relationships is to encourage shared activities. These shared experiences can provide opportunities for siblings to bond over common interests and create shared memories. Activities can range from participating in a sport together, working on a project, or even simply playing a board game. The goal is to create opportunities for positive interactions between the siblings.

Communication is another key factor in building strong sibling relationships. Encouraging siblings to express their feelings and thoughts to each other can promote understanding and empathy, helping to strengthen their bond. This can be achieved through family discussions or even through promoting one-on-one conversations between siblings.

Avoiding favoritism is also an essential part of building strong sibling relationships. Favoritism can lead to feelings of resentment and conflict among siblings. Therefore, it's important for parents to treat all children equally and fairly. This extends to all aspects of family life, including attention, praise, discipline, and opportunities.

Lastly, teaching conflict resolution skills can be invaluable in promoting healthy sibling relationships. Conflicts are a natural part of any relationship, and it's no different among siblings. However, teaching children how to handle conflicts constructively can equip them with the skills they need to navigate their relationships effectively.

Loyalty conflicts can arise in bonus families when a child feels torn between their biological parent and their bonus parent, or between their original family unit and the new bonus family. These conflicts can create stress for the child and disrupt the harmony within the family. Therefore, it's essential to navigate these conflicts with sensitivity and understanding.

Firstly, acknowledging the conflict and the child's feelings is an important step. It's critical to validate the child's emotions and reassure them that it's okay to have these feelings. This validation can provide the child with the reassurance they need to process their feelings without guilt or fear.

A crucial strategy in navigating loyalty conflicts is to avoid putting the child in the middle of any disputes or disagreements between the parents. Children should never feel like they have to choose sides or act as mediators. All parents and guardians, including those not living in the same household, need to commit to keeping the child out of any adult issues.

Open communication can also help to alleviate loyalty conflicts. Encouraging the child to express their feelings and thoughts can allow them to feel heard and understood. It's also an opportunity for the parents to provide reassurances and address any concerns the child may have.

Finally, it's important to reassure the child that loving their bonus parent doesn't mean they love their biological parent any less. Explaining to them that it's possible to have room in their hearts for all their parents can help to relieve any guilt or anxiety they may be feeling.

Creating unity amongst all parents and guardians in a bonus family is vital in building a harmonious and stable family environment. This unity can provide the children with a sense of security and consistency, which is crucial for their well-being.

One strategy for creating unity is to establish and maintain open lines of communication between all parents and guardians. Regular discussions about the children's needs, concerns, and daily routines can help to ensure everyone is on the same page and working together for the children's best interests.

Creating a co-parenting plan can also be an effective way to establish unity. This plan can outline the responsibilities of each parent, as well as expectations for communication and decision-making. Having this plan can provide clarity and consistency, which can aid in creating a unified front.

Lastly, it's important for all parents and guardians to show mutual respect for each other. This respect should be demonstrated not only in their interactions with each other but also in their discussions about each other with the children. Children learn from observing their parents' behaviors, so showing respect for all parents and guardians can model positive behaviors for the children and contribute to a respectful and harmonious family environment.

In conclusion, building relationships in a bonus family is a journey of patience, understanding, and respect. By employing strategies to foster bonds between bonus parents and bonus children, strengthen sibling relationships, navigate loyalty conflicts, and create unity amongst all parents and guardians, you can lay the foundations for a strong, harmonious bonus family. Always remember, every journey begins with a single step. Start your journey today and embrace the challenges and rewards that come with building a bonus family.

Action Steps for Chapter III

3.1 Reflection: Personal Journey Reflect on your personal journey within your blended family. Write down some key moments that stand out to you and consider what you learned from these experiences.

_____

_____

_____

_____

_____

_____

_____

_____

_____

_____

_____

_____

3.2 Research: Blended Family Dynamics Research more about the dynamics of blended families. What common issues do blended families face, and what strategies have been successful for them?

_____

_____

_____

_____

_____

_____

_____

_____

_____

_____

_____

3.3 Reflection: Parent-Child Relationship Consider your relationship with each child in the blended family. How have these relationships evolved over time? What factors influenced these changes? Write down your thoughts.

_____

_____

_____

_____

_____

_____

_____

_____

_____

_____

_____

3.4 Activity: Bonding Time Spend time with each child in the blended family individually, doing something they enjoy. This could be a hobby, a favorite game, or simply a walk in the park.

_____

_____

_____

_____

_____

_____

_____

_____

_____

_____

_____

3.5 Reflection: Listening Skills Reflect on your ability to listen to the children in your blended family. How effectively do you think you listen to them? How could you improve in this area?

_____

_____

_____

_____

_____

_____

_____

_____

_____

_____

3.6 Activity: Regular Communication Establish a routine for regular communication with all the children in your blended family. This could be a weekly family meeting, or individual chats where they can express their thoughts and feelings.

3.7 Research: Sibling Relationships Research strategies for fostering healthy sibling relationships within blended families. How can shared activities, equal treatment, and conflict resolution skills contribute to these relationships?

_____

_____

_____

3.8 Activity: Family Fun Organize a fun family activity that all siblings in your blended family can participate in. This could be a picnic, a movie night, or a visit to a local attraction.

_____

_____

_____

_____

_____

_____

_____

_____

_____

_____

3.9 Reflection: Loyalty Conflicts Consider if there have been instances of loyalty conflicts within your blended family. If so, how did you handle them? How could you navigate these situations in the future?

_____

_____

_____

_____

_____

_____

_____

_____

_____

_____

_____

3.10 Activity: Open Discussions Arrange for open discussions where children can express their feelings about the blended family dynamics, including any loyalty conflicts they might be facing.

_____

_____

_____

_____

_____

_____

_____

_____

3.11 Research: Co-Parenting Plans Research the concept of co-parenting plans and how they can create unity among all parents in a blended family. What elements should a co-parenting plan include?

_____

_____

_____

_____

_____

_____

_____

_____

_____

_____

_____

_____

3.12 Activity: Drafting a Co-Parenting Plan Collaborate with all parents and guardians in your blended family to draft a co-parenting plan. This plan should outline responsibilities, expectations, and methods for decision-making.

_____

_____

_____

_____

_____

_____

_____

_____

_____

_____

_____

_____

3.13 Reflection: Mutual Respect Reflect on the level of respect between all parents and guardians in your blended family. How can you demonstrate mutual respect more effectively?

_____

_____

_____

_____

_____

_____

_____

_____

_____

_____

3.14 Activity: Show of Respect Make a conscious effort to show respect for all parents and guardians in your blended family, both in your interactions with each other and in discussions with the children.

_____

_____

_____

_____

_____

_____

_____

_____

_____

_____

_____

3.15 Reflection: Your Bonus Family Journey Reflect on your overall journey of building relationships in your blended family. How has this journey influenced you personally? What challenges have you overcome, and what achievements are you proud of?

_____

_____

_____

_____

_____

_____

_____

_____

_____

_____

Remember, this is a journey and not a destination. Allow yourself and your family members the time and space they need to adjust and adapt to the new family structure. Patience, understanding, and respect will go a long way in making this journey a successful one.

CHAPTER IV

NAVIGATING PARENTING IN A BLENDED FAMILY

N avigating parenting in a blended or bonus family presents a unique set of challenges. It requires a delicate balance of honoring existing family traditions and norms, while also creating new ones that celebrate the formation of the blended family. Parents in a blended family need to contend with a variety of issues, such as different parenting styles, co-parenting strategies, and discipline practices.

Understanding and respecting that each family member may have different expectations and emotions about the new family dynamic is crucial. It's important to allow each person to express their feelings openly and honestly, and to validate those feelings. Remember, it's a transition period for everyone, not just the parents.

Growing up, I witnessed many friends and relatives contend with family structures that included 'outside dads' and 'inside moms'. The norm seemed to be a reluctance to allow anyone but biological parents to discipline children. These notions influenced my approach to parenting when I entered this blended family. I often found myself taking a backseat regarding discipline, motivated by the common perspectives about stepfathers, bonus fathers, or bonus mothers that I'd been surrounded by.

In the early days of our blended family, I frequently let my wife handle the disciplining of the children. This inadvertently created a dynamic where she was perceived as the 'bad guy', and I was the 'good guy'. While I never undermined her authority or coddled the children, it inevitably appeared as though I was the understanding parent, while she was the strict one.

As time passed, my wife voiced her concerns. She reminded me that I, too, was a parent, and couldn't always be the 'good guy'. She was weary of constantly being the 'bad guy'. Our conversations nudged me to reconsider my approach. I realized that I was apprehensive about overstepping boundaries. We were co-parents under the same roof, aiming to raise these children harmoniously. It was imperative that we disciplined consistently and were on the same page. Otherwise, the children could manipulate the situation, presenting different stories to each of us.

We traversed many hurdles, including the heartbreaking loss of our first biological child together early in our relationship. After this loss, we decided to bring a dog, Oreo, into our family. Unbeknownst to me, my wife used Oreo as a tool to help me hone my parenting skills. She cleverly employed the dog to foster conversations about what we would or wouldn't do as parents, allowing us to evaluate and align our parenting styles.

Our interactions with Oreo provided a unique backdrop for constructive dialogue and compromise. We learned to adapt and find common ground in our parenting techniques. These lessons carried over to our interactions with the children. The experience reiterated that life's lessons can be found in the most unexpected places.

Understanding your partner, their beliefs, and their intentions is crucial. Mutual confidence in each other's words and interpretations can greatly simplify co-parenting. There is always a lesson to be learned, sometimes we just need to use a 'dog' to see it.

Co-parenting in a blended family can be complex, especially when biological parents are living in separate households. The key to successful co-parenting is communication. All parents involved, whether they're living in the same household or not, need to establish clear, open, and respectful lines of communication.

Creating a co-parenting plan can be incredibly useful. This plan could outline key information, such as the children's schedules, important dates, medical information, and the division of parental responsibilities. Using a shared digital calendar or a co-parenting app can facilitate the sharing of this information and ensure that everyone is kept up-to-date.

It's also essential to present a united front as co-parents. Children can be quick to exploit discrepancies between parents' rules and expectations, leading to confusion and potential conflict. Consistency across households can provide a sense of stability and security for the children.

Blended families often bring together parents with different parenting styles and approaches. While this can present a challenge, it can also be an opportunity for growth and learning.

Open discussions about parenting beliefs and practices are crucial. Understanding why each parent approaches parenting the way they do can foster empathy and respect. These discussions can also highlight areas of alignment and areas where compromise or negotiation may be needed.

It's also important to remember that different doesn't mean wrong. Each parent brings their unique strengths to the parenting role, and children can benefit from being exposed to different ways of thinking and problem-solving.

However, in situations where differences in parenting styles lead to significant conflict or are detrimental to the children's well-being, seeking professional help, such as a family therapist or counselor, may be beneficial.

Discipline can be a particularly challenging aspect of parenting in a blended family. Parents may have different beliefs about discipline, and children may resist discipline from a bonus parent.

One approach is to let the biological parent take the lead on discipline, at least in the early stages of the blended family's formation. This allows the bonus parent and child to build a relationship without the strain of disciplinary issues. Over time, as the relationship strengthens, the bonus parent can gradually take on more of a disciplinary role.

Again, consistency is crucial when it comes to discipline. Children need to know that the same rules and consequences apply, regardless of which parent is present. This means that all parents need to agree on the key rules and consequences and commit to enforcing them consistently.

Establishing family meetings where rules and expectations are discussed can also be helpful. This gives everyone a voice, promotes understanding, and fosters a sense of collective responsibility.

In conclusion, navigating parenting in a blended family can be challenging but also incredibly rewarding. By establishing effective co-parenting strategies, navigating different parenting styles with respect and openness, and managing discipline in a thoughtful and consistent way, you can contribute to the well-being and happiness of your blended family. Remember, the ultimate goal is to provide a loving, stable environment where all family members feel valued and accepted.

Action Steps for Chapter IV

4.1 Reflection Activity: Analyzing the current parenting style

Write down your current parenting style. What influences have shaped this style?

_____

_____

_____

_____

_____

_____

_____

_____

_____

How do you handle discipline and why?

_____

_____

_____

_____

_____

_____

_____

_____

_____

_____

_____

What are your feelings towards your role in the blended family?

_____

_____

_____

_____

_____

_____

_____

_____

_____

_____

4.2 Research Task: Learning about other parenting styles

Investigate various parenting styles. Understand how they can influence children's development.

_____

_____

_____

_____

_____

_____

_____

_____

_____

_____

_____

_____

Discuss these findings with your partner. What do they think about these styles?

_____

_____

_____

_____

_____

_____

_____

_____

_____

_____

4.3 Reflection Activity: Sharing roles

Reflect on the roles each parent plays in the family. Are there any roles that feel imbalanced?

_____

_____

_____

_____

_____

_____

_____

_____

_____

_____

_____

_____

_____

How can you work towards sharing these roles more equally?

_____

_____

_____

_____

_____

_____

_____

_____

_____

_____

_____

_____

4.4 Action Task: Developing a co-parenting plan

Create a co-parenting plan with your partner and if applicable, the other biological parent(s). This should include key information like children's schedules, important dates, medical information, etc.

_____

_____

_____

_____

_____

_____

_____

_____

_____

_____

Consider using a shared digital calendar or a co-parenting app to help manage this plan.

_____

_____

_____

_____

_____

_____

_____

_____

_____

_____

4.5 Communication Exercise: Holding family meetings

o   Schedule regular family meetings where everyone has a chance to speak.

o   Discuss family rules, expectations, and any concerns or issues.

_____

_____

_____

_____

_____

_____

_____

_____

_____

_____

4.6 Reflection Activity: The role of discipline

Reflect on your discipline practices. How effective are they?

_____

_____

_____

_____

_____

_____

_____

_____

_____

_____

_____

_____

How do they affect your relationship with the children?

_____

_____

_____

_____

_____

_____

_____

_____

_____

_____

_____

_____

_____

_____

4.7 Action Task: Implementing consistent discipline

o   Agree on consistent rules and consequences with all parents.

o   Start enforcing these rules and consequences consistently.

_____

_____

_____

_____

_____

_____

_____

_____

_____

_____

4.8 Research Task: Seeking professional help

o   Investigate local resources for family therapists or counselors.

o   Consider seeking professional help if conflicts about parenting styles or discipline practices arise frequently.

_____

_____

_____

_____

_____

_____

_____

_____

_____

_____

_____

_____

_____

_____

4.9 Action Task: Building relationships

o   Spend individual time with each child to foster stronger relationships.

o   If comfortable, gradually incorporate more discipline practices as the relationship strengthens.

_____

_____

_____

_____

_____

_____

_____

_____

_____

_____

_____

_____

4.10 Reflection Activity: Reviewing your progress

Reflect on the changes you've made. Have they improved the family dynamic?

_____

_____

_____

_____

_____

_____

_____

What other changes could be beneficial? How will you implement them?

_____

_____

_____

_____

_____

_____

_____

_____

_____

_____

Remember, this is a journey. It is okay to make adjustments and changes along the way. The goal is to foster a loving and harmonious blended family environment.

CHAPTER V

OVERCOMING FINANCIAL CHALLENGES

O vercoming financial challenges is a significant aspect of ensuring harmony in blended families. The complexities of child support, alimony payments, and the management of household finances can create tension and conflict if not effectively addressed. Through open communication, clear planning, and the employment of stress-reducing strategies, blended families can navigate these financial challenges successfully.

Combining households invariably presents financial challenges, a reality Michael and I had to confront. Among these, child support for our four children was a particularly trying issue. After my divorce, there wasn't a system in place for child support for the first couple of years. Although we were entitled to receive support, it arrived sporadically, making it unreliable. Ideally, we could have allocated this money towards essential expenses, but due to its unpredictability, it often ended up covering minor costs like haircuts, takeout, or incidental groceries.

I later asked the court to automatically take child support from the children's biological father's pay as I hoped this would make the payments more regular and reliable. However, their father had inconsistent employment, so the payments continued to be inconsistent, which kept things unpredictable.

We grappled with several facets of this challenge. The unreliability of the payments, the insufficiency of the amounts, and the stark difference between what we received compared to others all added to our stress. Receiving sums between $250 to $400 every two weeks for four children often left us stretched thin.

Compounding these challenges were the frequent court visits, which were a source of additional strain. Nonetheless, having a supportive partner like Michael made this ordeal bearable. He did not get involved in the courtroom drama but offered unconditional support, playing the role of an empathetic listener and a comforting presence.

The onus was on me to relay the court proceedings to Michael, which he accepted with grace, understanding, and patience. He acknowledged that I had no control over the payment schedule and made a conscious choice to fully support our children, with or without the contribution from their biological father. He approached his role as a bonus parent with the full realization that his responsibility to our kids was not contingent on these payments.

There was one incident that proved to be unexpectedly beneficial. The biological father took me back to court, thinking his payments were too high. However, the judge ended up increasing the child support amount instead. Although this scenario baffled us, it was a welcomed development.

In a blended family setting, maintaining an understanding and non-pressuring relationship between the biological and bonus parent is critical. It eases the tension when the bonus parent does not pressure the biological parent to extract contributions from the other biological parent, which may be beyond their control. Such an understanding contributes significantly to the financial and communication aspects of the family, which are crucial elements in successfully blending a family. Patience, empathy, and an earnest desire to make things work for the family can go a long way in ensuring a harmonious blended family environment.

Imagine my surprise when Michael didn't take the usual drama filled route or use the opportunity to belittle the kids father. It was something unheard of in our community. People don't often take the high road or the hard road; it's definitely a road less traveled. It was another layer to understanding that he was in fact my person. Financial responsibilities are huge in any relationship but the expectation of the roles of the parents in blended families must be communicated clearly and with a realistic understanding of the whole picture.

As far as the child support was concerned, the amount Tyi was receiving was for four kids was laughable. I didn't have any experience besides hearing what friends pay in child support and on the outside looking in, I've never been in a courtroom, family court, you know, to go through the process or hear anything verbatim. And it seemed that Tyi had things well handled on the court side of things. So, I just chose to remain quiet. If asked a question on the subject, I would comment but, but for the most part, she seemed like she had things under control. So, I remained quiet and stayed the constant support system. If the situation required me to do anything beyond that, which it never did, I would have made the necessary adjustments, but I didn't have to. Tyi was so good, the kids didn't know anything was going on unless they were told.

The reality of child support and alimony payments can bring considerable strain. For the receiving parent, it may not feel like enough to cover the child's needs, while the paying parent may feel the financial pinch of these outgoings. Moreover, the arrival of these payments can create a sense of unease within the blended family, especially if the money's purpose isn't clearly understood by all members.

Open communication is essential to navigate this sensitive issue. If age-appropriate, it may be useful to explain to the children in a simple, straightforward way what child support is and why it's necessary. This can help alleviate any feelings of guilt or confusion they may have about these payments.

For the parents, it's important to remember that child support and alimony are legal obligations designed to ensure the well-being of the children. They are not a reflection of personal worth or parenting ability. If tensions arise over the amount of these payments, it may be beneficial to involve a neutral third party, such as a mediator or family law professional, to help navigate the

The management of household finances in a blended family can be more complex than in a traditional family structure. There might be different incomes, expenses, and financial obligations to consider. In some cases, there may also be disparities in the standard of living between the two original family units, which can lead to feelings of inequality.

A crucial first step in managing finances in a blended family is to establish a clear and transparent budget. This budget should take into account all incomes, expenses, and financial obligations, including child support and alimony payments. It should also consider the costs associated with maintaining any previous households, such as mortgage payments or rent.

It's essential to have open and honest discussions about money, including each person's attitudes and beliefs about finances. These conversations can be challenging but are vital in establishing a shared understanding and approach to managing money.

To tackle potential feelings of inequality, some blended families find it useful to pool their resources into a joint account for shared household expenses, while also maintaining separate accounts for personal spending. This approach can help ensure that household costs are met, while also allowing each individual some financial autonomy.

Financial stress can be detrimental to the harmony of a blended family. However, there are strategies that can help reduce this stress.

Firstly, maintain open communication about finances. This includes discussing any financial concerns or worries as they arise, rather than letting them fester and potentially lead to conflict.

Secondly, plan for the future. This includes establishing a savings plan for unexpected expenses and setting long-term financial goals, such as saving for the children's education or for retirement. Having a clear plan can help alleviate worries about the future.

Thirdly, seek professional advice. A financial advisor can provide valuable guidance on budgeting, saving, and investing, as well as on navigating the complexities of child support and alimony.

Finally, remember that financial stability takes time to achieve, especially in a blended family. Be patient with yourself and with each other, and celebrate the financial milestones you reach, no matter how small they may seem.

In conclusion, overcoming financial challenges in a blended family may seem daunting at first, but with the right approach, it's entirely possible. Navigating child support and alimony payments, managing household finances, and reducing financial stress are all part of the journey towards financial stability in a blended family.

In this journey, remember that every step you take is an investment in your family's future. Even the smallest progress is still progress. Each hurdle overcome is a testament to your resilience and dedication. And every success, no matter how small, is a cause for celebration.

Keep communication lines open, be honest about your concerns, and never hesitate to seek help when needed. With time, patience, and perseverance, your blended family can not only overcome financial challenges but also thrive in the face of them. As you navigate these waters, always keep in mind that your greatest asset is the love and unity within your family. With this as your foundation, there is no challenge too great to overcome.

As you continue on this journey, take it one day at a time. Celebrate the successes, learn from the challenges, and never lose sight of the love that brought your family together. After all, love, understanding, and respect are the pillars of a successful blended family - and they are also the best strategies for overcoming financial challenges.

In the end, the strength of a blended family does not lie in its finances but in its members. By working together, supporting one another, and facing challenges head-on, a blended family can overcome any financial challenge and build a secure, stable, and loving home. And that, ultimately, is the most rewarding investment of all.

Action Steps for Chapter V

5.1 Reflection Activity: Understand your financial situation

Write down your current income, expenses, and any financial obligations such as child support or alimony payments.

_____

_____

_____

_____

_____

_____

_____

_____

_____

_____

_____

Reflect on how your financial situation has changed since becoming a part of a blended family.

_____

_____

_____

_____

_____

_____

_____

_____

_____

_____

Write down any concerns or worries you have about your financial situation.

_____

_____

_____

_____

_____

_____

_____

_____

_____

_____

_____

5.2 Research Activity: Learn about budgeting

Research different methods of budgeting, such as the envelope system, the 50/30/20 rule, or zero-based budgeting.

_____

_____

_____

_____

_____

_____

_____

_____

_____

_____

_____

_____

Choose a budgeting method that you think would work best for your blended family.

_____

_____

_____

_____

_____

_____

_____

_____

_____

_____

5.3 Action Step: Create a Family Budget

o   Using the budgeting method you chose, create a budget for your blended family.

o   This budget should include all incomes, expenses, and financial obligations, including child support and alimony payments.

o   Consider using budgeting apps or tools to help manage your budget effectively.

5.4 Reflection Activity: Understand Your Beliefs about Money

Write down your beliefs and attitudes about money. For example, do you see money as a source of security or a source of stress?

_____

_____

_____

_____

_____

_____

_____

_____

_____

Reflect on how your beliefs about money might influence your approach to managing finances in your blended family.

_____

_____

_____

_____

_____

_____

_____

_____

_____

_____

5.5 Communication Activity: Discuss Finances as a Family

o   Schedule a family meeting to discuss finances.

o   In this meeting, discuss your budget, your financial goals, and any financial concerns you have.

o   Aim for openness and honesty in this discussion. It might be difficult, but it is crucial for financial harmony in your blended family.

_____

_____

_____

_____

_____

_____

_____

_____

_____

_____

5.6 Action Step: Establish a Savings Plan

o   Based on your family budget, establish a savings plan.

o   This plan could include saving for unexpected expenses, long-term goals like your children's education or retirement.

_____

_____

_____

_____

_____

_____

_____

_____

_____

_____

_____

_____

_____

5.7 Research Activity: Seek Professional Advice

o   Research financial advisors in your area.
o   Choose a financial advisor who has experience with blended families and schedule a meeting with them.
o   Prepare a list of questions or concerns to discuss during this meeting.

Here are some examples of questions or concerns you may want to ask your financial advisor:

1. How can we effectively merge our financial assets?
2. What should we consider when establishing a joint bank account?
3. How should we handle financial obligations to our children from previous relationships (child support, college funds, etc.)?
4. What are the implications for us regarding taxes?
5. How can we manage differences in spending habits or financial perspectives?
6. How can we save for retirement while still supporting our blended family's needs?
7. How can we set up an equitable inheritance plan that respects all of our children?

8. Can you provide guidance on the potential financial implications of legal matters such as custody or visitation rights?

9. What steps should we take to financially protect our family in case of emergencies or unexpected circumstances?

10. How do we handle healthcare expenses or insurance needs for our blended family?

11. How should we manage debt that was accrued before blending our families?

12. What is the best way to save for our children's education?

13. How do we prioritize our financial goals as a blended family?

14. How do we ensure financial transparency within our blended family?

Remember, these are just starting points. Your questions may vary based on your specific circumstances and needs.

5.8 Reflection Activity: Recognize your Progress

- o At the end of each month, reflect on the financial progress your blended family has made.
- o Write down any successes, no matter how small they may seem.
- o Reflect on any challenges you faced and how you overcame them.
- o Celebrate your successes and learn from your challenges.

_____

_____

_____

_____

_____

_____

_____

_____

_____

_____

Remember, overcoming financial challenges takes time and patience. Celebrate your progress, learn from your challenges, and keep communication lines open. With time and effort, your blended family can achieve financial stability and harmony.

CHAPTER VI

MANAGING EMOTIONAL CHALLENGES

In a blended family, emotional challenges can often appear as formidable mountains, casting long, unsettling shadows over the family unit. Jealousy, resentment, grief, loss, conflict, disagreements, and relationship baggage – these are just some of the complex emotions that can emerge in the blended family dynamic. However, with the right strategies, support, and understanding, these mountains can be scaled, and in their place, a landscape of emotional resilience and harmony can be crafted. This chapter will provide strategies to help blended families manage these emotional challenges, fostering a healthy and nurturing family environment.

Navigating the emotional challenges in a blended family can be a complex task, especially when the situation involves integrating five children with a man who previously had none. The complexities span various aspects, including devising parenting strategies, establishing routines, and imparting lessons, both good and bad. Children are like sponges, absorbing everything around them, and managing parental emotions alongside theirs is a daunting task.

Adding to the intricacy is the range of ages and gender differences among the children, necessitating an understanding of the unique needs of boys and girls at different stages. As a parent, you realize that there's no manual to follow.

You may present a strategy to your partner one day, only to observe its inefficacy the next, leading to an abrupt change. It requires a constant attunement to each child's needs and cues, a fluidity that can prove challenging to those unaccustomed to it.

Our children handled the divorce relatively well, though there were notable exceptions. One child reacted by vomiting daily for about four years, a physical manifestation of the emotional turmoil he experienced when his father moved out. Michael's understanding and willingness to listen, however, were invaluable during this time. He understood that my experience and knowledge could offer valuable insight into the children's emotional needs.

For instance, our boys needed physical expressions of affection – hugs, to be specific. This initially surprised Michael, especially considering societal norms around expressions of affection among males. However, when I pointed out how one of our sons would linger after saying goodnight, waiting for a hug that Michael had not realized he craved, a change occurred. Michael began hugging our boys daily, understanding the importance of such affection.

This example underscores the importance of communication, not only in understanding each child's needs but also in coordinating our parenting strategies. Over time, Michael grew to know the children so well that he often had insights I didn't, creating a beneficial reciprocity in our parenting roles.

In 2017, our family faced an additional emotional challenge when my ex-husband, was accused and later convicted of a serious crime. Discovering the news on Facebook was a shock, and I attempted to shield the children from the revelation. Our co-parenting relationship was already strained, and it deteriorated further after I started dating Michael.

Unilaterally, without consulting me, my ex-husband informed our children about his impending prison sentence. This revelation came within days of Michael and I discovering that we were expecting our youngest child. This reckless disclosure placed a significant emotional burden on the children, without considering the potential impacts or consulting with me.

When it comes to dealing with emotional challenges, it's an intricate, multi-faceted journey. It involves dealing with the past and the baggage it carries, and how it can profoundly impact present relationships. We literally say BAGGAGE in the middle of an exchange that we realize is being trigger by or because of someone outside of the room. Baggage, in this context, symbolizes past relationships, past hurt, and how these residual feelings could seep into our current relationships.

Both of us had been in long-term relationships before meeting each other. Consequently, we both carried our share of emotional baggage into our new union. Being aware of this baggage was critical, as was our ability to discuss it openly. We recognized that reactions triggered from past experiences or hurts were not about the person standing in front of us, but about something that transpired in the past. This understanding has been instrumental in helping us navigate through various emotional situations, allowing us to grow and strengthen our relationship.

Then there's the omnipresent shadow of death—an emotional situation that is perhaps one of the most challenging for anyone to navigate. Helping our children cope with the pain of losing loved ones, ensuring they understand their feelings, and creating a safe space for them to express their grief has been a complex task. It required us to muster our strength and support each other and our children, transforming the entire process into a communal learning experience.

Grappling with death is a deeply personal experience and varies significantly from person to person. We had to traverse this emotional landscape day by day, sometimes moment by moment, reassuring ourselves and the kids that it was okay to feel—to be sad, confused, angry. It was okay to cry, to talk about it, to remember, and to celebrate the lives of those we've lost.

Throughout these emotional challenges, communication has been the lighthouse guiding us through the storms. As partners, the conversations we have had with each other and with the kids have been crucial for our understanding and growth as a family unit.

This seventh chapter of our journey, managing emotional challenges, is a testament to our growth, understanding, and love. It's a journey we continue to embark upon, navigating every twist and turn as a family. As long as we maintain our channels of communication, as long as we understand and support each other, we can manage any emotional challenge that presents itself.

Ultimately, managing emotional challenges isn't just about coping with situations. It's about growing from them, learning from them, and using them to fortify our bonds, our relationship, and our family. This is what truly matters—the growth, the love, the family. It's what we strive for, every single day.

Strategies for Managing Jealousy and Resentment

Jealousy and resentment are common emotions in blended families, often stemming from feelings of insecurity, displacement, or fear of being overlooked or replaced. These feelings can be particularly strong in bonus children who are adjusting to new family dynamics. To manage these emotions, it's important to foster an atmosphere of acceptance, understanding, and reassurance.

Firstly, recognize and validate these emotions. Dismissing them can lead to further resentment. By acknowledging their feelings, you show respect for their emotional experience, making them feel heard and understood. Open dialogue about these feelings is essential. Regular family discussions, where everyone is encouraged to express their feelings honestly and respectfully, can be beneficial.

Secondly, ensure that every family member feels valued and included. Create opportunities for one-on-one bonding to reinforce their unique place in the family. Make an effort to celebrate each family member's individual achievements and highlight their importance in the family. These actions can help alleviate feelings of jealousy and resentment.

Supporting Children through Grief and Loss (Prison)

In blended families, grief and loss can be significant emotional challenges, especially if a biological parent is absent due to imprisonment. This loss can trigger a range of emotions in children, from anger and confusion to sadness and fear. As a bonus parent, your role is to provide a safe and supportive environment for the child to express and navigate these emotions.

Initially, it's essential to validate their feelings and empathize with their experience. Let them know that it's okay to feel upset, confused, or angry. Encourage them to express these feelings, either verbally or through activities such as drawing, writing, or role-playing. It's important to listen actively and provide comfort without trying to fix the situation.

In addition to emotional support, it's crucial to maintain a sense of normalcy and routine in their lives. Consistent routines can provide a sense of safety and predictability, which can be comforting during times of upheaval.

Lastly, consider seeking professional help if needed. Therapists, counselors, or support groups can provide additional resources and strategies to help children navigate their feelings of loss and grief.

Strategies for Managing Conflicts and Disagreements

Conflicts and disagreements are inevitable in any family, but in blended families, these can be more complex due to the added layers of relationships and dynamics. However, these conflicts can also be opportunities for growth and understanding.

Here are some strategies to manage conflicts effectively:

First, establish clear and respectful communication as a family norm. Everyone should feel comfortable expressing their feelings and thoughts without fear of judgment or reprisal. Encourage "I" statements (e.g., "I feel upset when...") to promote personal responsibility for emotions and actions, rather than blaming others.

Second, establish fair and consistent family rules. This can help prevent disagreements related to perceived favoritism or unfair treatment. Ensure that the rules are communicated clearly and that everyone understands the consequences of breaking them.

Third, consider implementing conflict resolution strategies such as taking a time-out to cool down, using active listening techniques, and seeking a compromise. Remember that the goal of conflict resolution isn't to determine who is right or wrong but rather to find a solution that respects and acknowledges everyone's feelings and perspectives.

Lastly, model respectful conflict resolution. As the adults in the family, you set the tone for how conflicts are handled. Demonstrating calm, respectful, and constructive conflict resolution can teach your children valuable skills that they can use in their own relationships.

Strategies for Managing Relationship Baggage

In blended families, relationship baggage - the lingering emotional and psychological effects of past relationships - can pose significant challenges. This baggage can impact how you relate to your new partner and children, potentially creating obstacles in building strong, healthy relationships.

One of the first steps in managing relationship baggage is to recognize and acknowledge its presence. Ignoring it won't make it disappear. Instead, it can cause you to unconsciously project past hurts, fears, or resentments onto your new family.

Once recognized, it's important to process these past experiences. This may involve exploring your feelings about past relationships, identifying patterns of behavior, and understanding how these might be affecting your current relationships. It can be helpful to do this with the assistance of a counselor or therapist, who can provide a safe, neutral space for exploration and offer strategies for healing.

It's also essential to communicate openly with your partner about your relationship baggage. Sharing your fears, insecurities, and expectations can help your partner understand your behavior and reactions better. It's important, however, to do this in a way that doesn't blame or criticize your partner but rather seeks understanding and support.

Finally, work on letting go of your past hurts and resentments. This doesn't mean forgetting them, but rather not allowing them to control your actions and reactions in your current relationship. This process may take time and patience, but it's crucial for building a healthy, fulfilling relationship in your blended family.

Managing emotional challenges in a blended family is a journey, not a destination. It requires patience, understanding, open communication, and a commitment to creating a nurturing, supportive environment. Remember, it's okay to seek help when needed, whether that's from a counselor, therapist, support group, or even a trusted friend. With the right strategies, emotional challenges can be managed, and your blended family can thrive, creating a unique family unit that is defined not by its challenges, but by its resilience, love, and mutual respect.

Action Steps for Chapter VI

6.1 Reflecting on Emotional Challenges

Reflect on a recent emotional challenge that you faced in your blended family. Write down the details, including the emotions you felt, how you reacted, and the outcome of the situation.

_____

_____

_____

_____

_____

_____

_____

_____

_____

_____

Consider if there was a more effective way you could have handled the situation. Write down any strategies or approaches you believe could have led to a better outcome.

_____

_____

_____

_____

_____

_____

_____

_____

_____

_____

Share your reflections with your partner. Discuss any strategies or approaches that you both could use in the future to better handle similar situations.

_____

_____

_____

_____

_____

_____

_____

_____

_____

_____

6.2 Understanding Emotional Baggage

Spend some time reflecting on your past relationships and experiences. Identify any emotions or issues that you may still be carrying with you ("emotional baggage").

_____

_____

_____

_____

_____

_____

_____

_____

_____

_____

Write down these experiences and the feelings associated with them. Try to identify any patterns or recurring themes.

_____

_____

_____

_____

_____

_____

_____

_____

Share your reflections with your partner. Discuss how these past experiences and emotions may be impacting your current relationship and family dynamic.

_____

_____

_____

_____

_____
_____
_____
_____
_____
_____
_____
_____
_____
_____

6.3 Managing Jealousy and Resentment

Have a family meeting where you discuss the feelings of jealousy and resentment. Make sure each family member gets a chance to express their feelings without interruption or judgement.

_____
_____
_____
_____
_____
_____
_____
_____
_____
_____
_____
_____

Write down key points from the discussion. Pay special attention to any patterns or recurring issues that come up.

_____

_____

_____

_____

_____

_____

_____

_____

_____

_____

_____

Brainstorm strategies to address these feelings, such as one-on-one bonding activities or celebrations of individual achievements.

_____

_____

_____

_____

_____

_____

_____

_____

_____

_____

6.4 Navigating Grief and Loss

1. Identify any recent experiences of grief or loss in your family.
2. Discuss these experiences as a family. Make sure each family member has a chance to express their feelings and thoughts.
3. Write down any strategies or activities that you think could help your family cope with these experiences, such as maintaining regular routines or seeking professional help.

_____

_____

_____

_____

_____

_____

_____

_____

_____

_____

6.5 Resolving Conflicts

Write down any recent conflicts or disagreements in your family.

_____

_____

_____

_____

_____

_____

_____

_____

_____

_____

_____

_____

_____

Reflect on these conflicts. Were they resolved effectively? If not, what could have been done differently?

_____

_____

_____

_____

_____

_____

_____

_____

_____

_____

Discuss these reflections as a family. Come up with a list of conflict resolution strategies that you can use in the future, such as using "I" statements, taking time-outs, and seeking compromises.

_____

_____

_____

_____

_____

_____

_____

_____

_____

6.6 Seeking Support

1. Reflect on your emotional challenges and the strategies you've been using to manage them.
2. Do you feel like you need additional support? This could be in the form of a counselor, therapist, support group, or a trusted friend.
3. Research available support options in your area and write down any that you think could be helpful for your family.

_____

_____

_____

_____

_____

_____

_____

_____

_____

Remember, managing emotional challenges in a blended family is a journey. These activities are meant to provide you with tools and strategies to help you navigate this journey. However, they are not meant to replace professional help if you or your family need it. Don't hesitate to seek support when necessary.

CHAPTER VII

CELEBRATING DIVERSITY IN A BLENDED FAMILY

A blended family is a beautiful mosaic, a dynamic and vibrant blend of diverse backgrounds, traditions, and experiences. It's a unique space where different cultures, religions, and identities intersect, creating a rich tapestry of diversity. However, this diversity can also present its own set of challenges, as individuals navigate their unique identities and strive to find a sense of belonging within the new family structure.

In this chapter titled "Celebrating Diversity in a Blended Family," we delve into the intricacies of fostering harmony in a culturally and religiously diverse blended family. Our journey begins with the crucial step of recognizing and respecting each family member's unique cultural and religious differences. It's an essential foundation, setting the stage for a respectful and empathetic family environment.

From there, we move on to explore how to actively celebrate this diversity, transforming potential challenges into opportunities for growth, understanding, and unity. We'll discuss practical strategies for integrating various cultural and religious practices into everyday family life, thereby creating a shared family culture that cherishes diversity.

Finally, we address the vital task of building a strong sense of identity and belonging. Amid the confluence of diverse backgrounds, each family member—especially children—needs to feel seen, acknowledged, and valued for their unique identities. Simultaneously, it's necessary to foster a shared family identity, a sense of unity that binds the family together.

Navigating the diversity of a blended family may seem complex, but it's an enriching journey that can strengthen the bonds between family members and create a truly inclusive and harmonious family environment. This chapter aims to be your guide on this rewarding journey, providing insights and strategies to help you celebrate the beautiful diversity of your blended family.

This chapter revolves around the celebration of cultural diversity in our family—a theme that was not as disparate as it may seem. Michael's inclusion in our family wasn't a mere blending of cultures, but a harmonious merge into our traditions—our church visits, our birthday celebrations, our holiday festivities. As a man without children stepping into a household of five kids, Michael had a unique challenge. However, he never saw us as a ready-made family unwilling to incorporate him. On the contrary, he was lovingly accepted and became an integral part of our family.

I often ask Michael what made him stay, despite the odds and the inevitable chaos of a large family. His response always revolves around our shared celebrations and traditions—our unique blend of Barbadian, Panamanian, and American culture from my side, with his Jamaican and Haitian roots. Despite the cultural differences, the commonalities were significant, which led to a deeper understanding of who we were individually and as a family.

The kids were fascinated by Michael's heritage and bombarded him with questions about Jamaica and Haiti. Their intrigue showcased the common ground rather than the differences, bringing more diversity and richness to our family culture. We didn't meticulously dissect the distinctions; we embraced what was similar, what worked well, and what could be potentially added to our traditions.

When Michael joined our family, it was crucial to establish that our family traditions wouldn't entirely mimic those with their biological father. However, there were few rituals to undo. This lack of set traditions allowed us to set the tone and precedent for our family moving forward. The kids' trust in us as parents made this transition seamless and comfortable.

Celebrating cultural diversity extends beyond our family. We've observed families with differing religions such as Muslim and Jewish, Christian and Muslim, and how they harmoniously celebrate all the holidays on their respective calendars. Such situations add an extra layer of love, reinforcing the idea that respecting cultural differences and understanding varying perspectives is vital.

Honoring the differences, the similarities, the new and old is the best approach to managing cultural diversity. Central to all this, as always, is communication. Miscommunication can be one of the toughest challenges in blending a family, especially in understanding what was said versus what was understood. Nurturing the kids' understanding of their identity and their place within the family is also essential.

In our family, we've seen our kids find their unique roles. We have a daughter who brings all the Christmas spirit, a son who has evolved from being emotionless to brimming with emotion, constantly working to keep the family together. It's heartwarming to watch them grow in their roles.

From Michael's perspective, blending cultures in our household was a seamless process. Being Jamaican, Haitian, and American and marrying into a family with Panamanian, Costa Rican, and American roots, we shared a Caribbean culture. Our children have become more culturally aware, curious about their parents' cultural histories, and teaching each other about their diverse heritages.

We've embraced cultural traditions, especially those centered around family. Now our daughters switch between Spanish and English accents, mimicking what they've heard and learned—a testament to their cultural immersion.

In conclusion, our cultural blend was one of the easier aspects of our journey, enriching our family dynamics, fostering a deeper understanding, and nurturing our collective growth.

A blended family is a microcosm of our diverse society, often bringing together individuals from different cultural, ethnic, or religious backgrounds. Recognizing and respecting these differences is the first step towards celebrating diversity in a blended family.

In a blended family, it is crucial to approach cultural and religious differences with an open mind and a respectful attitude. This involves actively learning about each other's traditions, customs, beliefs, and values. For instance, you might explore each other's cultural practices, celebrate each other's religious holidays, or learn each other's languages. By doing so, you not only show respect for each other's backgrounds, but also create opportunities for shared experiences and understanding.

However, respecting cultural and religious differences also means acknowledging that these differences might sometimes create conflicts or misunderstandings. It's important to approach these situations with patience, empathy, and a commitment to dialogue. Open and respectful discussions about these differences can lead to mutual understanding, compromise, and even growth.

Once you've recognized and respected each other's cultural and religious differences, the next step is to actively celebrate diversity in your blended family. This involves creating a family culture that not only tolerates diversity but embraces and cherishes it.

One way to do this is by integrating each other's cultural and religious practices into your family routines. This could mean incorporating food from different cuisines into your meals, incorporating elements of different religions into your family rituals, or celebrating cultural holidays together.

Another way to celebrate diversity is through education. This could involve learning about each other's cultures or religions or studying about different cultures and religions as a family. This not only broadens your understanding of the world but also fosters a sense of curiosity, openness, and respect for diversity.

Remember, celebrating diversity isn't about assimilating into one culture or religion, but about creating a family culture that values and cherishes each individual's unique background and beliefs.

In a blended family, building a strong sense of identity and belonging can be a challenge, especially for children. They may feel torn between different cultural or religious identities, or struggle to find their place within the new family structure.

To help children navigate these challenges, it's important to foster an environment where each individual's identity is recognized and valued. This involves acknowledging each child's unique background, experiences, and beliefs, and encouraging them to express and explore these aspects of their identity.

At the same time, it's also important to cultivate a shared family identity. This involves creating shared experiences, traditions, and values that unite your family, while also acknowledging and respecting each individual's unique identity. This balance between individual and collective identity can foster a sense of belonging, unity, and mutual respect within your blended family.

Finally, remember that building a strong sense of identity and belonging is an ongoing process, not a one-time event. It requires patience, understanding, and a commitment to nurturing each individual's growth and development within the context of your blended family.

Celebrating diversity in a blended family is a journey of exploration, understanding, and growth. It involves recognizing and respecting each other's cultural and religious differences, actively celebrating these differences, and fostering a strong sense of identity and belonging. By doing so, you can create a blended family that not only tolerates diversity, but embraces it, creating a vibrant, enriching, and loving family environment.

Action Steps for Chapter VII

7.1 Recognizing and Respecting Diversity:

Research Activity 1: Ask each family member to share some vital aspects of their cultural or religious background. Look up these traditions, customs, and values to gain a better understanding.

_____

_____

_____

_____

_____

_____

_____

_____

_____

Research Activity 2: Create a "family map" of cultural and religious origins. This can include the country, main traditions, popular dishes, and unique customs.

7.2 **Celebrating Diversity**:

Research Activity 3: Each month, focus on celebrating one cultural or religious tradition that is part of your family's diverse background. Involve the whole family in planning the celebration to ensure everyone's input and engagement.

January _____

_____

_____

February _____

_____

_____

March _____

_____

_____

April _____

_____

_____

May _____

_____

_____

June _____

_____

_____

_____

July _____

_____

_____

_____

August _____

_____

_____

_____

September _____

_____

_____

_____

October _____

_____

_____

_____

November _____

_____

_____

_____

December _____

_____

_____

_____

Research Activity 4: Search for books, movies, or documentaries that highlight the cultures and religions present in your family. Plan family movie or reading nights to enjoy and discuss these together.

_____

_____

_____

_____

_____

_____

_____

_____

_____

_____

7.3 Building a Sense of Identity and Belonging:

Research Activity 5: Investigate the concept of "cultural identity" and how it forms. This will help you understand the processes your children are going through as they negotiate their identities in the blended family.

_____

_____

_____

_____

_____

_____

_____

_____

_____

_____

Research Activity 6: Look for resources and advice on how to create a shared family identity, such as shared values, goals, and traditions.

_____

_____

_____

_____

_____

_____

_____

_____

_____

_____

7.4 Recognizing and Respecting Diversity:

Reflection Activity 1: Reflect on how you felt when learning about each other's cultural or religious practices. Were there any that particularly intrigued you or challenged your beliefs?

_____

_____

_____

_____

_____

_____

_____

_____

_____

_____

_____

Reflection Activity 2: Discuss instances where cultural or religious differences might have led to misunderstandings or conflicts in the family. How were these resolved, and what was learned from these instances?

_____

_____

_____

_____

_____

_____

_____

_____

_____

_____

_____

7.5 Celebrating Diversity:

Reflection Activity 3: After each monthly cultural or religious celebration, reflect on the experience. What did you enjoy? What did you learn? How did the experience bring you closer as a family?

_____

_____

_____

_____
_____
_____
_____
_____
_____
_____
_____
_____
_____
_____
_____
_____
_____
_____
_____

Reflection Activity 4: After each family movie or reading night, have a discussion. What did you learn from the movie or book? How did it increase your appreciation for the particular culture or religion?

_____
_____
_____
_____
_____
_____
_____
_____

_____
_____
_____
_____
_____
_____
_____
_____

7.6 Building a Sense of Identity and Belonging:

Reflection Activity 5: Reflect on the identities that each family member is forming. How can you as a family support the growth and evolution of these identities?

_____
_____
_____
_____
_____
_____
_____
_____
_____
_____
_____
_____
_____

Reflection Activity 6: Reflect on the shared family identity that you are cultivating. What are its key elements? How does it encompass and respect the diversity within the family?

_____

_____

_____

_____

_____

_____

_____

_____

_____

_____

_____

_____

_____

_____

_____

CHAPTER VIII

CONCLUSION: CELEBRATING THE JOURNEY OF BLENDED FAMILIES

As we draw this guide to a close, it's important to reflect on the multifaceted journey we've embarked on together. We've navigated the intricate landscape of blended families, delving into the myriad challenges they face, and illuminating strategies to overcome them. The aim has always been singular - to foster harmonious, resilient, and happy blended families. In doing so, we've recognized that the path towards creating a successful blended family is, indeed, less of a destination and more of an ongoing journey.

What a journey this has been! The most beautiful aspect of this life we lead is indeed the journey itself. Life, in its incredible diversity, brings different pieces and experiences to the table, teaching us to dance in the rain and appreciate the joy in the storm. Joy and fun are cornerstones of our household, even amid the COVID pandemic that brought unprecedented challenges but also unexpected blessings.

The pandemic has been an eye-opener in many ways—it intensified our communication, allowed us to understand each individual within our family more intimately, and reiterated the profound truth that our children come through us, but they are not ours. They are tiny humans with their own set of feelings, realizations, and life situations. Every child is unique, and no two kids, even with the same parents, share the exact experiences or perspectives.

With each child, we as parents learn something new about ourselves and about them, further broadening our horizons. The beauty of a blended family lies in this continuous process of learning and evolving—it's an additional layer of love, a bonus, if you will. A bonus parent, bonus piggyback rides, bonus car rides, bonus vacations, bonus in-laws, aunties, uncles and grandmas.

Blending a family isn't just about the merging of two units—it's an added layer of richness, a bonus in our lives. It should be seen as a good, a great thing, rather than a challenge. If it's perceived as anything other than that, it ceases to be a bonus and instead becomes a burden, which isn't what family life should be. Of course, we understand that family life can be tumultuous and unpredictable, and things don't always work out as planned. But leading with intention, clear communication, and understanding can go a long way in ensuring harmony.

Clarity and intent have been our guiding principles. It's essential to truly comprehend what the other person is saying or trying to say, without letting interpretations cloud the message. One of the most critical communication skills in blended families, and in life in general, is to listen—not to respond, but to genuinely hear what's being said.

Regular check-ins and open conversations within the family are also vital. Celebrating the good times, working through the rough patches, and growing together—these are the aspects that make the journey worthwhile. This journey of blending, of bonding, and of building our unique family has been one of the most gratifying experiences of our lives.

We began by understanding the unique dynamics and challenges of blended families, underlining the importance of acknowledging these hurdles in order to confront them effectively. From defining the roles of bonus parents and bonus children to addressing the emotional and financial challenges, we've explored the vast terrain that blended families must navigate.

We emphasized the importance of a strong foundation, recognizing that the bedrock of a successful blended family lies in creating a shared vision, clear communication, and realistic expectations. We looked at strategies to foster strong relationships between all family members, and the crucial role of effective co-parenting. We also delved into the complexities of managing different parenting styles and approaches, and the importance of consistency in discipline.

Overcoming financial challenges, often a significant source of stress in blended families, was another key topic. We discussed practical strategies to navigate child support and alimony payments, manage finances within the family, and methods to reduce financial stress.

The emotional challenges within blended families, including jealousy, resentment, grief, and loss, were addressed with empathy and practical advice. We stressed the importance of supporting children and adults alike through these emotional transitions and presented strategies to manage conflicts and relationship baggage.

One of the most beautiful aspects of blended families, diversity, was celebrated in-depth. We explored the importance of recognizing and respecting cultural and religious differences, and how to create a strong sense of identity and belonging in this diverse family setting.

In revisiting these key strategies and tips, it's important to remember that every blended family is unique. What works for one family might not work for another. The real success lies in your family's commitment to learning, growing, and evolving together, in creating a loving and understanding environment where each member feels seen and valued.

As we wrap up, let's take a moment to appreciate the extraordinary journey of blended families. It's a journey of courage and resilience, of learning and unlearning, of embracing change and growing together. There's no denying that it's challenging, but it's these very challenges that make blended families such a testament to the incredible adaptability and strength of human connections.

The journey of a blended family is, indeed, a celebration. It's a celebration of love that transcends traditional boundaries, of resilience in the face of change, and of the beautiful diversity that enriches our lives. As you continue on this journey, remember to celebrate every step, every challenge overcome, every bond formed.

And above all, remember that you are not alone. There's a vast community of blended families out there, each with their unique stories, struggles, and successes. Draw strength from them and, in turn, inspire others with your journey. The path of the blended family is complex and challenging, but it's also immensely rewarding, filled with endless opportunities for growth, love, and unity. Keep moving forward, keep growing, and keep celebrating. Your blended family's journey is a story worth telling.

Thank you for embarking on this journey with us. We wish you nothing but success, love, and happiness in your blended family's ongoing adventure.

ABOUT THE AUTHORS

Tyi and Michael are a dynamic duo who share a passion for building harmonious, resilient blended families. As founders of Blissfully Blended Academy and authors of "The Blended Family Blueprint," their mission is to provide practical strategies and a supportive community to foster understanding, communication, and connection within blended families.

Brooklyn-born Tyi holds an Associate of Arts degree from New York College of Technology and a Bachelor of Sciences in Psychology from the College of New Rochelle. Besides being a daughter, sister, wife, and mom, she is also a Certified Birth Doula and Childbirth Educator. Raised in a blended family from the age of four, Tyi has personal experience with the unique challenges and joys that come with this dynamic. Her first and second marriages further broadened her blended family experience, giving her profound insights into the nuances of managing such families.

Michael was born in Brooklyn but grew up in Queens, NY. At 12, his family moved to Fredericksburg, Virginia, where he stayed until he turned 18. After attending Virginia State University, he returned to NY and began a career in healthcare. Michael is a son, brother, husband, uncle, godfather, and friend who brings a wealth of practical and personal experience to their joint venture.

Tyi and Michael met at work, and what started as a fun friendship evolved into the perfect partnership and the bedrock of their blended family. Affectionately referring to their marriage as "THISTHING," their journey together humorously started without labels. But the absence of labels turned into a life-long commitment that has not only shaped their family dynamics but has also fueled their dedication to supporting others on a similar journey.

Their mission with Blissfully Blended Academy is to create a comprehensive platform that empowers blended families. They aim to provide the tools, resources, and community needed to navigate the complexities and celebrate the unique beauty of blended family life. Their core belief is that every blended family, with the right guidance and support, can become a beacon of love, resilience, and harmony. Through their book, "The Blended Family Blueprint," and Blissfully Blended Academy, Tyi and Michael are passionately dedicated to guiding blended families on their journey to a blissful and fulfilling family life.

www.ingramcontent.com/pod-product-compliance
Lightning Source LLC
Chambersburg PA
CBHW070720130626
46553CB00005B/2078